The Devil Gets Lonely Too

The Devil Gets Lonely Too

Poems by
Thomas R. Langton

Matador
9 Priory Business Park,
Wistow Road, Kibworth Beauchamp,
Leicestershire. LE8 0RX
Tel: 0116 279 2299
Email: books@troubador.co.uk
Web: www.troubador.co.uk/matador
Twitter: @matadorbooks

ISBN 978 1788038 843

British Library Cataloguing in Publication Data.
A catalogue record for this book is available from the British Library.

Printed and bound by CPI Group (UK) Ltd, Croydon, CR0 4YY
Typeset in 10pt Minion Pro by Troubador Publishing Ltd, Leicester, UK

Matador is an imprint of Troubador Publishing Ltd

This book is dedicated to the underbelly of society and everything that makes it tick

Contents

Devils In The Night

Got another story to tell
I've sunken to new lows
Oh well
Maybe I shouldn't dwell

It'll lead me into the pits
I'll only lose my wits
And she's having a fit!

Cause we were devils, devils in the night
Looking for easy meals, with the right deals
When I get home find her writing them letters
Better not be addressing my betters
Shooting them notes off to Neville

He knows, he knows I'm a foul old devil that Neville
Begging you, I'm begging you don't meddle

She caught me in the alleys with her sister
I'm sorry but I just couldn't resist her

Lipstick marks on our sheets
Broken promises left in the streets

Missus got real bitter
But I just can't quit her

Now she's growling when I'm out prowling
It ain't no feat just my regular beat

Watching the sun go up
When the moon goes down
Watching the sun go up
When the moon goes down

Caught in the alleys
An I'm gonna be another exhibition
In her shooting galley

Got another story to tell
Maybe I shouldn't dwell
It'll lead me into a pit
I'll only lose my wits
And she's having a fit!

Cause we were devils, devils in the night
Holding my wallet close holding out for the corner man's snow
For when the smiles will flow

Looking for easy meals, with the right deals
Looking at the shows, ready for the blows
Because Neville knows, Neville knows
Will we come to blows, when she knows?

2

When she knows
We were devils in the night

Romily

Where shall I begin?
Girl, I've been missing that evil grin
Might just push you down this rabbit hole
Sell my soul just to see you
Back in that rabbit hole

You were quiet as a mouse
With a flick of a switch
And I see you sprouting things
Now you got horns, you got wings
Suddenly you're voracious, audacious, flirtatious

Drop the amp, so you can
Come & play with me Romily
Oh won't you come & play with me Romily
I know, I know you won't
It leaves my heart ticking sombrely

Isn't she lovely?
I want her back
I know it's not likely
And I've been missing that evil grin

Might just push you down the rabbit hole
Sell my soul just to see you
Back in that rabbit hole
Quiet as a mouse
With a flick of a switch
See you sprouting things
Now you got horns, wings, and a forked tongue
Suddenly you're voracious, audacious, flirtatious

Drop that amp
And come & play with me Romily
Oh won't you come & play with me Romily
I know, I know you won't
It leaves my heart ticking sombrely

Don't force me to scream down these hatches
Tell me, tell me where the fuck are you now!
Romily! Romily! Romily!
Sweet, sweet heavy child
Won't you please come back?

Devil's Village

Immortal kings, queens & the god damn senate too
Who will you be?
Will you play the tyrant or the villain?

Angels are just a pipe-dream
Foul minions play with dying fowl
And demons just won't do
They had to send devils too

This isn't sacrilege
This is just a pagan's patronage

Now should my heroes be
Deprived of this stage
But all these rogues
Wrapped in silk & velvet
Seem to be
Depraved enough for you

The woodland sorcerers left battered & bloodied
The poets of war
Don't play on the battlefields

Dead kings don't go marching
When the neophytes are calling

Robed figures took her in the night
She's from Salem
They said she's just a corner store whore
But I know
She's from the hilltop
Now she's Moscow's bitch

They built themselves
Temples to these wooden fools
As you lay siege to their golden idols
Worshipping the corrupt ghouls
Now I see you sitting atop your own Devil's shoulder
Hissing your plots
Planting the seeds
As the pyre calls

One of these days the children will go marching
On your Devil's Village
Till they're brave enough
To walk through the smokescreen
To reach your Devil's Village

This legion of piss soaked
Blood stained generals will assemble
At the gates of your kingdom
Built atop my forefather's skulls and thrones
Laid beneath these tombs of sandstone

7

Sons of liberty
Stand fast
Before your brothers of war
This tower will crumble a thousand times
But we'll pick up the pieces as the fire flies

Now I confess; Odin met Zeus, and Hera too
Does Nemesis know, you're my nemesis?
The Devil isn't sitting on my shoulder
I suspect you sit on his instead.

Beautiful Irish Bastard

He just couldn't slay that urban beast
A beast on the hunt
For love, lumps & lust
Valentino clashed with Johnny
For a dirty tail or two
To end the night black & blue
Stumbling on back through the Clifton Grange
He promised her it was just a phase
Oh, mama! Oh, mama!
Boys will be boys
Those rogues are so damn vogue

Mars is brooding over Venus
We don't give a damn if the public eye has seen us

Sitting here in mourning
For a man I never knew

I'm dropping my needle on that twin axe attack
I'm telling you it's
Sgt. Rock's twin axe attack

So Irish, that boy forgot to be black
Up to no good on the streets of Moss-side
Could have been Harlem
But it had to be Crumlin-side

Made it past twenty-seven
But never in with the specials
It's a right old ghost town
Troubadours made a good impression
But they're dead by eleven
Club closed early, & we're cut up from a bad line up
We were too damn aggressive
Banned from the strip and I'm left in a fit of depression

I've got to speak up now that
The roars of the crowd are gone
And I'm standing here
Edge of the stage, wondering

Will you remember these songs?
Will you remember my words?
Will you remember us?
Will you remember me?
When the spotlights gone

We're looking at you
Telling you, asking you
When I'm looking in the mirror
Please, don't mistake this insecurity for vanity
The crowds used to bring me sanity

But now they're gone
And the silence is even more deafening

I'm still here on stage
Alone, and feeling empty
When the spotlight has gone

Monsters At The Wheel

Smile, fry & die
The pearly toothed monsters need you
Crooked cops, with silky white shirts & mustard stains

Mascots are drained from their presence
They look at them like peasants
Fighting over the dying pheasants
On the hunt for one last meal
Pearly toothed monsters
Will smile, fry & die

Mascots uplift our morale
And the cheerleaders will flaunter
But it won't last long

The working Joe breaks his foot
As the laughing Arthur collects his pay check
This ain't what he wanted but it's what he got
Well this is what you get
When monsters are at the wheel

Smile, fry & die
My girl's got cancer
I don't have the heart to say goodbye
She can't pay for the poison
But I can pay for mine

I'm just another damn monster
Pearly toothed, suit-clad monster
Counting paper, tossing silver, eating copper

Somebody stop 'em
Before this burning world
Eats its oil, as we toil and recoil
At the horrors of the cities we built

Monsters at the wheel
Checking his reflection in the rear view mirror
Blood on his paper
Oil in his hair
Whitener on his fangs
Silky, velvety fine fabrics from China
Alloys from Venezuela
The children got sciatica
No health-plan just a 24-hour suicide net

Smile, fry & die
You best enjoy the little things
The diamonds & gold
Come at a cost
The oil doesn't come without the toil

But green sure does smell good
He flies by the floods, stepping over the mud
He doesn't see it, but you know he must
He extends his hand, with a grin

Won't you please shake his hand?
We're all just pearly toothed monsters
Driving at the wheel
Monsters are at the wheel

You can see it, but does he?
Are your eyes with me?
Do you see the horizon?
The cliffside approaches
But this isn't our stop
Pearly toothed monsters'
We'll all smile, fry & die

Ballad Of The Spaniard

Spring was in the air
Love is fair but it's mine to bear
She wore white, I wore grey

Something's missing and my
Rose pin's itching
Doesn't matter
Here she comes
Down the aisle
Of the pretty little chapel

We're here for the day
For our big day
Petals to metal
As that organ sings her chorus

White clad brown woman
Don't you do no wrong
You can't do no wrong
In that beautiful white dress

White clad beauty
I told you, you don't need no stinking veil
I'm proud, proud, proud to stand here
This damn male has only got you now
He ain't leaving you
Till we may depart

The sun hasn't set
And my brothers ain't no threat
Love is fair but they promised
Revenge is in store
There ain't no justice when you're poor

Do the bells toll for them, or us?
What time is it?
The band ain't playing
And the family sure ain't paying
Bells keep on tolling
And my brothers are withholding
One last round

Your dress, your beautiful dress
I'm sorry, I'm sorry my love
You've ruined your pretty red dress
Today won't be ours
Don't cry dear
Lay still dear, and please don't fear
We'll get through it
We'll be together

Brothers, brothers
You couldn't, you shouldn't
Brothers, brothers please
Save the last round
You can have it all
Brothers, brothers
Finish it all

Brothers, brothers
Please, save the last round for me

California Rock Queen

She was on her last dollar bill
Low on money, self-esteem, & something worth living for
Well Jaime never could share
So she fucked him right over
Does she regret it? Does she hate him?
Does she wish, does she wish?
She could change it all?

Something worth fighting for never showed its face
Will it ever stop raining down in California?
Nothing a new town, nothing a new job,
Nothing a new fella will change
Jaime can fuck right off with those bitches

I'm gonna go on down
Right on down to the boulevard
Play my heart out, play my hatred out
Paint these dirty streets gold
With love, new-found on the streets of Hollywood

I know I'm just some crazy fool
Hoping for something new

I might just be crazy enough
To attract the right kind of crew

Well, down in California
It only takes a one night stand
To flip a coin from orphan to the prince of sunshine

We're playing on the beaches
Playing in the parks
Playing & rocking for the stages
For the great many faces
Who believe in us

I'll just dance till the rains are gone
Till my baby comes peeking round that corner
And one day I'll be her mother

The only mother I need
Is a six string, flicking with her pick
Ticking down to the next show
In front of the screaming joys of the crowd
As it washes over me
Washes over me like a fresh day

What I needed more than another dollar
This rain's turned green
Sand, surf, and pretty gleaming smiles everywhere I turn
Boy you better smile

What're you crying for?
Don't you know I love you?
We can dance
Oh yes we can dance
And later tonight I'll be in your pants

This is just a nightmare & will soon be over
This is just the dream of another California Rock Queen
And she's gonna fuck you over

Meet Me On The Mountain

Meet me on the mountain
Under the stars
I'll fall for you
With a wicked spell
You'll be mine & I'll be yours
When the night is ours
And the moon shines high

I'll run barefoot through the woods
Burning cabins & farms
So I can meet you on the mountain
Lost & in love
Running from the world
So long as you
Meet me on the mountain

Serenade me under fresh moonlight
Till the morning comes
And they find me sleeping in the river
I won't care, I won't care
So long as you play with me

Play with me under red starlight
Till the blood runs black
And the smoke comes back
I'll be waiting for you
Knocking on my door

Hold me against the floor
Doing whatever you do

Under the river
I'll love you
On snowy peaks

No matter what
Meet me on the mountain

The First Girl I Never Had

I've got rips in my jeans
And some girl is staring
I know she's seen it
But still those pretty blue eyes gleam and shine
And she shoots me with a wicked smile
Does she care?

I've emptied my pockets, and now I'm all done, moneys
Dried up
She said she'd sell her silver locket
I say no, she says yes
She's not the first, but she's got my number
Quenching my thirst on those pink lips
She leaves the tips, staring at my rips, letting my fibs slide.

Baring my soul in her glare
Do I dare?
It just ain't fair
I'm in an emotional flare
And my hearts tearing it
Way on down, to a final goodbye kiss

Every time I think back to the first girl
The girl I never had
The first girl I never had
I'm glad I don't remember
But it doesn't hurt, thinking back
And how many more
Smiles, lies, and eyes will I forget?

The first girl I never had
Where are you now?
Do you remember?
Do you want to remember?
Do I even want to remember?
No, no, no.

The first girl I never had
Blue eyes, brown eyes, grey eyes, hazel eyes.
Black hair, blonde hair, red hair.
Whoever, whatever, wherever you are.
What's your name?
I just can't remember.
Did it happen in September, November or December?
I spotted you, you spotted me.
And that was that.
We never talked, you never talked, and I never gawked.
It's too late for us now.

The first girl I never had
Won't you please forget me?

My Wild West

Last man standing takes the gold
The boys only want silver, but the sheriff just won't fold

Dust in my eyes as the train blows past
The regal madame catches my eye as we blast

Waiting for the boys, they're hollering for eight
They'll be late, and the outlaws will have lost another fate
Escaping the strait, and the fools dropped another crate

Blood soaked floor in the saloon
Whisky shots for high noon
Can we make the trail?
Will mother post my bail?

Sally won't look me in the eye, she caught me with Allie
I promise I'm on my way back up through the valley
The natives are on our backs
The deputies watching the banks

Another girl's got one in the cot
She loved me when I was shot

I'm sorry Sally, Sally please
She's just a passing tease
Never meant to hurt you
But I love you too

I've been hit in the chest
Blood all over my vest
Save me from this bugle calling
This life is forestalling
I know you don't care
But please offer me a prayer
I loved her, but I still love you
Don't let our love fall through

She kept me on my toes, she was my Wild West
But you're my beautiful Southern Rose

Don't let it end like this
Give me one last kiss
Before they drag me off & bury me in the abyss

Set Sail

Set sail off into the distant shores
To the stars of yesterday, and tomorrow
Voyaging into the black, never stopping for wars

His compass long lost
Flying onwards across
Space, an infinite treasure trove
Any port at his call, a secret cove

The riches revealing sights untold
And in this time of man, one must be bold

Gun at the ready for the hunters
Light-speed reveals all of the wonders

And he'll stop at nothing for the thunder
To reach the exquisite plunder

Life goes on, and on in an endless sea of stars
The nights left for hunger, and laughter

Days not more than poor
But it's these tales of yore
That we fight for

Caged

A woman trapped
Eternally engaged
She aches for release
Calling to the winds

Across the ages
He hears her
The pain echoes
The earth trembles
The wind speaks to him

He can't find her
His heart is shattered glass
She wants to pick up the pieces
But she is frozen

All that they are
Both calling
Both deaf

One day they will hear
And rescue each other

When Devils Dance

A full moon hangs high
Its midnight at the masquerade
Lovers sway at the ball
But she is all alone

Suitors lost in a trance
They're all caught
In her beautiful glance
Dusk offered but dawn declined

Who dares ask her hand, but a perfect gentleman?
Does such a man exist?
A twinkle in her eye under the night sky

A perfect gentleman catches her eye
But he isn't a prince
A mysterious stranger he is

And he takes her hand
She doesn't know how to say no
He's a rogue
Through and through

She doesn't know
He's the almighty
The true & first fallen angel

He tells her gently
But she just doesn't care
She quivers under his breath
Pleading to the stranger

'Oh, won't you please
Tell me all about your days
And your frightful ways
Tell me while we're on stage'

But under the moonlight
The devil entices
In the gardens they go

Where the devil may dance
Where the devil may in trance
He made a perfect entrance

She whispers softly to him
Pleading & begging;

'Serenade me Satan
Oh won't you please
Serenade me please'

The summer rains come
And love may unfold
When devils dance

Strange

Is it strange
To do things alone
To drink alone
Go the movies alone
See a band alone
Go on holiday alone

People will call you weird
People call you loser
People call you strange

Are they right?
Or are they just scared?

People who can't be alone
They are the strange ones to me

I don't like being alone
But I don't dislike it either

Making friends might be easy
Keeping them isn't

Isn't it strange?
The ones who call us strange
Are the strangest of all.

Knock, Knock Juliet

He was a winter urchin
She was a spring beauty
Two twisted souls entwined
In the thorns & aromas of summer

When that boy came calling
In the dusk of autumn
Giving me stage fright
Soothing me with his soft touch
His deep voice calling
Oh don't you know
My Romeo came calling

He's dark and perverted
He's a demon alright

When that girl came knocking
In the dawn of my mourning
She sang, she sang;
'Come and play with me Romeo'
Juliet came knocking
Oh that girl came knocking

She's cute & innocent
She's an angel alright

They go out
Dancing and falling
All over each other's feet
Awkward is as awkward does

One day stood up
Next day, made up
Living from week to week
Our knee's both weak
What the hell does that guy seek?
What's that girl's deal?

They hit the café rouge
He swore he'd never fall for
Bleu ou rouge

Now the sunlight fades
They know what they never knew
And time reveals

They both see it all
He's an angel
She's a demon

A guy comes knocking
'Knock, knock Juliet'
A girl comes beseeching

'Open up Romeo'
Courting done right and wrong

It never mattered what
Their song said
Only that their song was sung

Pretty Boy

All my life
All I've ever heard is
You're a pretty boy
Handsome, & ruggedly good looking
But

Maybe
I don't want to be pretty
Beauty can be a burden
Why else do all those celebrities
Die so young?
The world watching them
Judging their every move
They're so pretty but act such a fool

It's always the ugly
The old, ugly, fat and bald men
Old men with faces like cracked teapots
The ugly annoying idiots
Who get the women
How do they do it?
Confidence & charisma
Come easy to these guys

But the young, good and handsome
The ones with the perfectly chiselled faces
Filled with fear & dread
Insecure, and panic

I never asked for this
Wouldn't it be better
Surely it would be better
To be ugly
To be unseen

I feel their eyes on me
Constant, fluttering eyes
Winks and smiles
It makes me so tired

Moon

Moon
A full moon
Hanging high
Full, fat, & blue

Its nightly visage
Haunting me
The quiet of the twilight
Utterly daunting

The stars flaunting
Sparkling & shimmering
Bringing the dawn
When the last
Bird has flown

Oh Dear, Oh Deer

'Oh dear…' I said
'I'm going hunting for some deer'
'Don't be too long my dear' she spoke
'Don't be too long now pa' said the children
'Oh dearies, don't worry I shan't be too long'
'It's only a deer, after all'

'We do need the food on our plate'
'And the kids will think it's so great'
'I won't be very late'

'But dear, be careful'
'That rifle is dangerous' she said

'Oh dear the rifle is fine'
'Wait for me by the fire'
'And enjoy the wine'

Hmm, oh dear
It does appear
My dear was right
This rifle's sight isn't quite right

There goes the deer
Spooked and in a tremble of fear

Careful now
Slowly now
Along the forest now

A shot
A miss
A cuss

The damn rifle's sight
Gave us both a damn fright
And the deer is nowhere
In my sight
Must have taken flight

Rustle, rustle, rustle
Oh dear
Where is that deer

Reload
Quickly, and quietly now
Oh dear, where is that deer?

Rustle, rustle, rustle
Charge, pound, and fall
Oh dear, there it is
That damn deer
I guess I won't
See my dear
After this damn deer

Look who should have had
The fear
It surely wasn't that damn deer
I hope someone tells my dear
'Goodbye my dear'
Thanks for nothing
You damn deer

Nowhere, Somewhere, & Everywhere

I wanna go
Nowhere
Somewhere
& everywhere

Someplace nobody knows my name
Nowhere where I know
A place to lose myself
Where I can get lost
And just wander
Through forests
Over the mountains and hills
And under the stars

Sleeping rough
Feeling good
Looking like shit
Approached by no-one
Nobody but the wind
The rain, the sunshine, & moonlight

Navigating by touch, smell, and taste
Following my soul
To the darkest, and lightest
Deserted places
Fighting society with sheer wanderlust

I wanna go everywhere
And nowhere
Just somewhere
Guitar on my back
Books at my feet
And the birds, and breeze
As my only symphony
A sonnet & saga of nature
Breezing past me
Through me
And into me

I wanna be alone
Walking off into the dirt roads
Swimming off into the horizon
Never to return

To find nothing
And everything
If I return
Will you go back with me?
I wanna show you nowhere, somewhere, & everywhere

Shit-Show

Your poetry is too generic
They said
It's got no rhythm
It doesn't rhyme
Too many lines

You've got no discipline
It's amateurish
It's too vulgar
You swear too much
It just hasn't got that flow

They say this, and that
It just falls a bit flat
Well drat, excuse me
But I wasn't looking for
You to pat me on the back

Honestly I don't give a shit
If it doesn't fit the classes rules
You idiots are obsessed with
Some dead writer's creed

Pawing at each other like goddamn animals
For some worthless appraisal

I write what I like
If you like it too
Then maybe it
Was worth it
For the few
Who appreciated the sentiment

But really, who gives a shit?
This is just a shit-show
It's a no-go
I'll find my flow
When you piss off, fuck off
And let me grow
In my own time

This is my generic shit
And I'll admit
It is a total shit-show
And that's okay
Cause I'm just learning
To stand on my own
And put up with myself

One day maybe
My shit-show
Will be worth a shit

Muse

I need a muse
Oh you could be that
And so much more
Would you like to be my muse?

They say every writer, every poet
Every artist, every artisan
Had their muse
A beauty there for the inspiration
For heartache
For pain, love, lust and death

I've never had my heart broken
And I want you to be the first
Won't you please rip this beating heart
Out of my chest
Lick it, eat it, and fuck it
Stomp, spit and throw my heart away

I need a pretty little blonde
With ice blue eyes
An evil brunette

With eyes of fire
A demented redhead
With eyes of jade
Who's not afraid
To set me on fire

Someone to love and leave me
Leave me spiralling and falling
Tumbling through the dark
Make me feel alone in the brightest day

And maybe one day
I'll feel that hole
In my heart
Recover

But my heart is whole
And I'm forever being told
You ain't anything without pain
Your writing won't make it
So I keep faking it

One day that muse will appear
Kiss me, love me, & leave me
With blood all over her hands
And a gaping hole in my chest

Collapsed on the floor
Clutching my missing pieces
And then, finally
I'll whisper to the world

Why?

Whore

I spent my night with a whore
I always promised myself that I wouldn't
But I did it anyway
It wasn't love
Hell, it was barely even lust

But she was beautiful, blonde & fair
And I just didn't care
About blowing my wad & last pay-check
On a girl that wouldn't even remember me

I don't feel the guilt-trip
Everyone places on me
But maybe it's too early yet

I think I'll see her again
That beautiful whore
I really want to spend my night
With that beautiful whore

The Vagabond

I came before your gods
& their gods too

I consulted the old sultans
And advised the princes
Well beyond your years
I was around before this mighty empire
I've conspired, retired, & fired
Nations greater, and lesser than this
You see me as the poor pauper
But I was around when Genghis fell
& the Huns won

I stared into the eyes of Jupiter as I plunged my knife in
Julius Caesar
I'll never forget the hate-filled gaze
He shot me
Such a soul-broken leer

When Constantinople became Istanbul I stood
By their side, looking long fully
At just another throne

The thousand crowns
I have fitted
Upon a hundred heads
Of rulers; great, and small
Just, and true
Pious, and holy
Mad, and barbaric
Some worthy, and some lost to their own folly

And you are none so cruel
As any who have come before
The great many monarchs prayed
Before and afore me
They begged, they wept, and they confessed
At my feet

Each full of joy, and sorrow
Hiding and parading
In the corners and corridors
Of their palaces, castles, and kingdoms

The world shall retain, all of the rulers
Who are vain, untamed, and slightly insane
But you mustn't, and shouldn't
I warn you now

Don't believe that which you have been taught
Your democracy is a lie
The great theocracies were bitter bile
This life is nothing but a trial

You are the one who may be judged
But the board is engulfed
In their own minds, sins, and personal flings
They're too busy, preoccupied, & clearly
In need to be rectified
To soundly judge your corruption
They may revile, you and your crime
But I assure you they are only thinking of their own
Precious time

After a while, they will forget
The world shall forget
All the things you did
Believe me, I should know
For my shadows, skeletons, and demons run deep
My tales run on, and some ever do don
A life of their own
My secrets could fill the caverns of the earth
Like lost & hidden treasure troves
Overbearing, and overburdening
With secrets alive and dead
Mine, and others from back down the line
I have seen and foreseen
It all before

There is nothing of past lives I have not seen
And I truly wish I could have shut my eyes, & mind
To have never seen the great tragedies, of lives past
The casualties I have seen, met and fled
I was the cause

For I am the original
The catalyst
The ever great doom

I stood and watched the fast fires of Rome
As I stood in the shadows of Nero
I conferred with Plato
Of the hemlock, I did serve
I gazed at the great wooden horse
I guarded lovers & siblings alike from public so foul
Watching over Cesare & Lucrezia under ashen cowl
I attended parisian balls at the behest of Louis, himself
I rolled die and placed checkmate on Henry after the trials
I witnessed the rise and dear demise of Persia
Carthage, & Babylonia too

I am the aeons made flesh
For I am, were, and was

The instigator, the great inciter, and shadowy strider
The depraved low witted deceiver
The bane, and dread
Of Europe, and Asia

I survived the plagues, quakes, and storms
And lived to dine with the last kings, & queens
Paupers, and whores, prophets, & slaves

But it has never been enough
I go on and on and on

Living, and dying endlessly
Sighting, and enticing
Any of the great who shall greet me
It doesn't matter how they treated me
They are gone now, whilst I, still live

I often stop, and ponder, whenever I see a new wonder
Shall the world ever see the things I saw
Civilization and society gave me
A rumbling anxiety, in its million-chance variety
This tale I weave is my final sobriety

I go far away again, in search of something new
To find someone true, none of the beings I met
Ever had the slightest clue

Now in my sojourn
I recall, everything
Every lesson, every mistake
Every person, every people
Every city, every nation
Every friend, every lover
Every enemy, and every acquaintance
Every event, every battle won & lost
Every piece of peace, and all the wars
And the sieges that broke the mightiest walls
Out of it all, I remember it all
The loudest, and quietest
The kings, and queens
The priests, cardinals, and popes

The sultans, shoguns, and shahs
The killers, kaisers, and khans
The caliphs, chiefs, and caliphates
The eunuchs, dancers, and jesters
The whores, beggars, liars & cheats
The poets, artists, and actors
The emperors, and their ghastly empires

Each and every one of them a sheer fool
I know it all, and I am the only one to have seen
Them both stand tall and see them fall
I am over it all, and my soul
Now lies crippled, broken and torn
I shall go back to where I once came from
In a land long gone, from mind, book, and thought
No map may know where I might freely crow
Back to simple things, where I can grow, & sow
Upon that little farm, in no-one's land

Back to where
I might have once been born
In a land forlorn and far gone

27

27, and you're only still young
Sometimes I feel this youth
That is upon me
Other times I feel the age
Creeping up on me

Am I young or old?
Only time will tell me
The days fly by
And I seem to do nothing
Staring at dry walls, for hours on end
Thinking of the times I have fallen
Never how I could fly
Or how I should get up and try

Wasting hours, days, months and years
Before I slept I was 18
After the short sweet sleep
I was 27

Where will I be after another short sweet sleep?
I never thought I'd make it to 27

I never made plans to get past 16
But now I am indeed 27
27, and still so young
Feeling old, weary, and wounded

Really, do I need to get past 27?
27 is a good age
And it has felt like an age
Life feels like nothing but a tight cage
27, and no plans

Planning to reach 30
Just sounds vile and dirty
I want to stay forever 27

The Highway

We're all just clones
Travelling down this highway of life
Fucking, loving and hating
Till we make clones again of ourselves
It's a piss poor excuse
But you'll keep on going forward
Shifting gear
Till one day you reach the end of this road
And crash, flung from your seat
Rolling around, covered in blood
Holding your guts in
Till you're completely fucked
And done

Portrait

The heart of a poet
The face of a drunk
Personality of a wet paper cloth
Cracked smile
And eyes of the damned
He's complex
But it's a rare glimpse for him to flinch
He'll devour you
Maul, and enthral you
All in good time little girl
Have some patience
He'll make his way to your door
When he's good and ready
Whenever that is
Eventually

I See Red

I see red, whether good or bad

She smiles, giggles, and flirts
I see red
My blood pumps slightly faster
A lump in my throat, and I can't speak
I can't think and I see red
She makes me see red

I see red, whether good or bad

That asshole at the bar, cut me off
No more liquor, that barman
That prick cut me off
I see red
I clench my fist
My blood pumps faster
That bastard, makes me see red

I see red, whether good or bad

Lovelorn

I can't help it if I'm lovelorn
Everywhere I look there are roses
But everywhere I step there are thorns
I feel like someone's pawn
In some cruel chess game
I get taken out by the simplest misstep
And overtaken by another rook

Three-Step Emotion

When the world seems so cold
And both sexes get so lonely
Women will want a good reaction
Men just want some sweet interaction

And when you're alone
The world seems so dark
When you spend too much time reflecting
You'll find your happiness when you finally
Spend some time...

...Connecting
And stop overreacting

Women

Women
Beautiful, & wicked
Life's greatest
Intrinsic mystics
Wrathful, spiteful
& bashful
One day they act the jackal
Next day flutter, and stutter
Innocent, and chaste
When they get a taste
Promiscuous, & ambiguous
When they assemble
And suddenly you tremble
But some damsels
Are worth the gamble

Masquerade

I took my mask off a long time ago darling
But I still keep it close, for when I'm feeling morose
I've worn it for my entire life, and several others
Society is a like a forgotten, dusty, bottle of spirit
It can stay on the shelf for decades, and centuries
Once opened it begins to sour, and if left unchecked
Dropped, chipped, smashed or shattered
It can leak all over you, spilling its dull-witted poison
That's when you wear the mask, and you better keep that mask
But don't dare wear it too long, it'll only mould into your soul
And soon, you'll forget it was just a mask
And you won't be able to remove it
Moderation is the key
Wear it often when in doubt of the demons at your back
But not too often for the angels in your face
If you abuse this mask, it'll only crack and will
Become you, ensnare you, envelope you
And then you will stop, unable to use that mask
No longer able to revel, and the fools will see you true
And then you'll be among them
Another fool dancing at that ball of life
Unable to dance, with your own eyes, and smile

With genuine delight, gone, your heart will blacken
In that beautiful fake ball
That we all dance for

The Exile

(I)
There's a romantic fool in my heart
He seeks the eternal harlot
I curse him out with rhythm & blood

(II)
The moon is low, the sun is high
Now I take my respite in shallow ground
Only at dusk shall I rise

(III)
A mortal love awaits in that hallowed town
He carries thorned roses by his side
I could hold his heart in the palm of my hand

(IV)
My immortal queen resides inside
Her cold touch is my truest lust
She is a sweet & dead obsession

(V)

That child of time awakens me
I see him and greet him
And rip him limb from limb

(VI)

My black soul undone
I hold a beating heart
And breathe deep of the roses he brought

Owning The Muse

A page a day
Keeps the muse in chains
Where she should be so lucky.
Keep that beautiful harlot
In her personal cell;
At your desk
In your mind
And longing for you
As you long for her.

Drunken Horses

Drunken horses feast on hungry lakes
The gods of the black marsh
Dancing & revelling in their bloodlust
On the fiery shores of tomorrow

The sins of the saved redeem the damned
And the temples lay scattered and lost
Throughout the cities the immigrants built
On the blood, bones, and burial grounds of
Those who came before

Ale flows down rivers of gold
Wine rains down on us
And we bathe in the poison
All around us

Smothering, and breathing in
Their culture as we wave our burning flags
Screaming & spitting our vile bile

Drink the coffee, down the beer
Sip the wine, savour the whisky

Gulp the tea, gasp as the food
Is brought to you on silver platter
Making you and your mind that much fatter
Forget the tip
They didn't earn it
Carry on, carry on
Keep calm
And keep on keeping on

We're all drunken horses
Passing by the blackened dead lakes
Laughing, and dancing around the gods gone by
Lying on the fiery shores
That we never even spilt blood for
These shores are ours now
And we will dance, fuck, and love
Like they always were

Drunken horses
May live and quiver
For we may live forever
Dancing forever with drunken horses
With us… The drunken horses

The Suicide Drifter

He was born under a December moon
Loved & cherished by all
Under snow & cloud, thunder, and rain

The boy named Phil, oldest of two
Mother's favourite – father vacated
Sister; Natalie, she died at two

A great childhood despite the misery
Mother faked her smile all those years
Lost child – deserted husband
She kept herself in check for her Phil

Well Phil had plenty of friends
A good laugh here and there
School easy and good
Holidays, experiences, and a lot of love
An easy youth despite the misery

Teenage years come and flicker
Flicking the switch for good happy Phil
He lost and found new friends

Moving home and city
School rough and gruff
First day bullied, unsure of it all
Phil had friends but it didn't matter much
Bullied, teased, and abused
Each day a fight, struggling to avoid it all
He played & skived, ignoring teachers & work
One day passing with flying colours
Next day the class clown
Got in fights, and cried in his late nights

Grandmother, uncle, and grandfather dead
Doesn't matter kept his chin up
Kept his head down as he passed the bullies
Day to day, week to week it didn't work
It made him sick
Dizzy, lightheaded and refusing to eat
Suicide looked good, but guilt kept him around

Graduation came and past
Lost contact with those friends
Never made any more
Failed the tests, deciding what to do
Was nothing but a pest
Got into college
Studied hard, standing & sitting alone
Sapped of confidence
Filled with anxiety, paranoia, & pessimism
Lost the weight, couldn't put it back on
More idiots came and went

Offended but never pretended
Ignore them Phil told himself
They don't know anything he told himself

Couple of years pass Phil and he's still alone
No friends, girls, or loves
Got a job, was only part time
Stayed there too long
Moved on

He drifted from city to city
Lost contact with those he knew
Poor old mum, didn't hear much of Phil
She got cancer, died in hospital
He missed the funeral and processions

Nearing thirty not much changed
Phil lingered and got fingered for a police charge
Spent some time inside, cried, and tired
Couldn't keep that chin up
Suicide looked good after a thought
Tried and failed, he was tailed by the guards

Let out and let loose
He hung a noose
Neighbour saved him and told him
Make your peace with life
You'll see something good
You just gotta make truce with your past
Phil tried but it didn't last

74

Another city, another attempt
The suicide drifter drifted
A hundred schemes, jobs, and failures
Homeless, friendless, jobless, womanless
The drifter a vagabond, robbing in the alleys
Shooting the junk up
Holding his gun up
And weighing his life up

Well it's tough, but what else did Phil have?
Cross country, cross-atlantic, sun-surf – rain, snow
No matter where, his heart teared
His soul numb, his mind hollow and gone
Phil the lowlife suicide drifter
Travelled the world
Dying mentally each and every night
And spewing up his guts in the morn
Hangovers vicious and quite viscous

The barrel of his gun tasted good
But it always jammed
The noose tight but always too loose
Pills a load of shit, Phil just spewed them up

Well, Phil the suicidal drifter drifted
One place, to second place
Never looking back
Was he cursed or blessed
He couldn't decide

One day bottled, next day burned
Caught the cancer but was cured
Did god hate or love him
He wasn't sure if he believed in any of it

Forty and living it rough
Renting a trailer
The whores looked him down
Pimps hunted him down
Addicts beat him
Tricked and never treated
Black & blue but never finished off

Phil, the suicidal drifter fifty
Sixty & seventy
Piss poor and fucked up
Shot up, stabbed and bones broken
A life of high mileage
Nothing to show for it

Eighty and done with it
Tired, racist, abusive and demented
Left in a rotten care home and neglected
Spending too much time reflecting
Till the reaper came

Phil survived broken hips, legs, skull fractures
Pissing the bed, shitting his kecks
Drooling at the breakfast table
Young ones laughing

Old ones snoring
Phil couldn't speak up but heard and seen it all

Phil reached one hundred
Phil, the suicide drifter immobile
Just wanted someone to end it
Refusing medication, food, and drink too

Fuck it all, he thought
'I'll survive it all'
'I have before…'

Next night Phil died
It was a beautiful sunny day
Nobody came to claim him
Phil, the suicide drifter dead
Finally, happy

Puzzle

I told her a while ago
That she was easy to read
She said I was hard to read
I realise now what a gigantic fuck-up
That was on my part
As the more I picked her mind
The more I realised what was there
More and more layers unveiled themselves
She was a wonderfully complex puzzle
And I just couldn't solve it
Couldn't fit the pieces into place
And by the time I did
By the time I'd finished that
Wonderful puzzle
It came to me
I had it all wrong
The puzzle was upside down
I thought she liked me
And I didn't like her
I turned the puzzle backwards to make it forwards
And discovered;
I liked her

And she didn't like me
I swore, moaned and banged my fist against the puzzle
And threw it back in its beautiful cold box
And tried my best to forget it was there

Words Are All I Have

I have nothing to offer you but words
I'll quench my numb hungry soul
On the words of those who've came & passed me by
The rhythm, and spirits on offer
And maybe if you're ready
I could get this heart to beat again
If not for you, then maybe for myself

Words are all I have
And I could lend you them
For a time
I could give you... Words
It's up to you whether they mean anything

Anything – anything, at all

Scars For You

I have scars
Scars on sale
Scars for you
Scars for hire
And some to spare
You can have them all

Beat The Blood

Beat the blood
Out and into him
Rib splintering & fast
He didn't pull any of those punches
Jaw shattered, nose broken twice now
Leg throbbing and limping
Knuckles blue and beating the floor

All four come at me
I'm done & fucked
The biggest ones always have the knife
Spit in his eyes
Punch to the sternum
Slap to the throat
Elbow to elbow
Foot to his knee
He drops down hard

The bigger they are the harder they fall?
No, fuck that noise
The bigger they are the harder they hit

Beat the blood
Spit, piss, & blood
Snot, and a little shit too
Only a fool isn't scared

Keep your cool
Don't rush in like a fool
Breathe, stay cool
And think

Beat his skull, before he beats yours
Break his hand, legs, and arms if you have to
Anything to keep these bastards down

Beat the blood
Out and into him
Before it's into you
This is gonna be a long night
Win or lose
Eyes of fire
Eyes of water
Shaky lips
Trembling fists
Coughing up spit
Spitting out teeth

One down, two and more
I hit the floor
They stand tall
I'll crawl
I don't care at all

Beat the blood
Stand up and stand tall
Eyes of fire

Eyes of water
Fuck 'em all

I'll beat the blood
Out and into him
Win or lose
I'll beat this blood

The Cunt From Lunt

A boy from Lunt
Raised on Mercury
Smitten and fixated on the great
Mercury

Hard Rock called to him
The rock – the rock & roll
Called to that boy
Posters all over his walls
Of that rock god
Mercury

Idolised and praised
Calling out to the skies
Air guitar, head banging and a total rush

Queen, British and proud
That boy loved Queen
Freddie Mercury his idol
Totally and completely

That boy turned a man
Saw all the music-videos
Had the collection
Saw some shows
Toured and dedicated for Mercury

A boy became a man
A man from Lunt
And Mercury broke free
Freddie was free
Freddie broke free

The boy… stopped
Shaken & stirred
Traumatised
In denial, but soon
In anger and fury
Tore down the posters
Smashed his records
Sold his tapes

And damned the man
That beautiful man
Freddie, oh Freddie
Don't you know that boy
That boy loved you
Freddie… that boy loved you

That man hates Freddie
That boy grew up

And shrunk down
Love askew & the idol gone
His obsession corrupted

That man... damned and cursed
Mercury

Mercury broke free
And true colours fly
Hate & bitter bile
Shame & utter denial

That cunt from Lunt
He hates Mercury
The cunt from Lunt
Oh don't you know Freddie
That man hates you

That cunt from Lunt
Even after it all
After all the years
That man from Lunt
That cunt... he still hates you
Freddie...

Why did you have to break free Freddie?
Didn't you know?
That boy loved you Freddie

You're A Crank

Don't tell me to smile
I have nothing to smile for
What are you smiling for?
Yeah, well ain't that good for you

I'll smile when I want, when I can
When there's something worth smiling for

It's a chemical imbalance
And I can't help it
It's the anxiety & depression
Plus the other shit too
Loneliness, isn't it fun?

I'm grumpy, cynical
Pessimistic – nihilistic
Introverted & pissed off too

Creativity gives you plenty to play with
But robs you of the regular normal things
A common skillset in everybody's hands
Just isn't in my arsenal

Socially inept – if you keep up with
That chitchat
I'll keep hearing nothing but bullshit
Pouring forth out your mouth
It just makes me want to walk away
Or slap you right in that stupid face

I'm sorry, yeah I'm a bit cranky
Maybe I'm just tired
Maybe I'm hungry
Maybe I'm in a mood
Maybe it's the anxiety
Maybe it's the depression
Maybe it's the bitterness
I don't fucking know
But I just can't deal with you
Or this at all right now

Give me a little time
I'll be fine – in a little while

Whisky, Books, & Whores

All I need to get me
Through this life is;
Whisky, books, & whores

I learnt how to walk
But I still crawl when I can't stand
I'm used to the fall
Falling is second nature
More so than breathing
It comes easier
I can fall more naturally
Than I can suck air up into these lungs

Jobs, friends, & girls
Are a headache
I don't have them
Need them or want them

All I need to get me through this life
Is whisky, books, & whores
Till I reach my last fall
And crawl into that

Fucked up hole
Next to the last asshole who fell
Then you can cover me with dirt
And forget you buried me here

Just give me;
Whisky, books, & whores
It's all I can bear

Misery

Misery is my coat of arms
They said; 'you've got such sad eyes'
'They look so far off, and distant'

Misery is my drug
My booze – my liquor
My poison and supplement
It's a plaster to cover the numbness
And I'll inflict heartache to refresh it
All over again

Happiness tastes bitter
It's foreign and excruciating
Like the rays of light blinding you
In a foul hangover

Give me misery
It's my coat of arms
Give me misery
It's my holy water
My aqua de vida
My chalice to sip & gulp

Pour a little heartache over me
And I can revel all night long
Spoon feed me some happiness
It's a shock to the system – No

Give me misery
It's my coat of arms
I'll let it devour me

Give me misery
And I can spin you a tale
I could weave you legends
Myths, & legends for eternity
Just give me what I need

Pour a little heartache over me
Give me misery
And I could dazzle you

Please – oh please
Give me misery
It's my coat of arms

The Monk Of Funk

Damn that boy could jive
Twist, n' dance – curl & jive
He played the funk, rock – blues & soul
Funky ole creole right on down through his soul

Sit & listen, he'll give you goosebumps
Feel the hairs on your arms flinch
And your feet thump, your ears cringe
A funky tinge'll run up your spine
Reach in your pockets and dig deep
That boy – that boy, he plays the funky ole junk

Your heart will sink, you'll forget about your drink
He's a maestro, artisan and a master craftsman
The monk of funk, real ole good funk
He plays the good ole creole

That boy with a wild heart
Untamed, and not for the plain
Twist n' shout, curl n' jive
Rock your head, click your thumbs
Beat your feet, drum those hands

Here he comes, that monk
That monk of funk
Playing true gold
Talent untold
He's the blues personified
The great shade in the dark haze
A silhouette in the dark, with a perfect mind set

Give it up for him ladies & gents
Dig deep, for him
He's here and this is his new lair
Ending the night with a mad damn flare
Playing that good ole creole
For your lost soul
Bless him he did impress you
Curl & whirl – Jive and cry
He's so damn fly
That monk – that damn monk
That monk of funk

Monsters

We play on fields of fire
With monsters and cattle

Dining on blood and bone
Pour that fire into his cup

He'll drink it down
He's depraved, enflamed, and ever…
So insane
A monster through and through
But only for you

The monsters walk city streets
Feasting their eyes on your delicate treats

They could step along so playfully
For all of eternity

Looked up and down as gods, and demons
Saints, and brutes – Monsters absolute

May sun shine on your back
And moon far from you

How far he could traverse
Till she would converse

Convert – And join the flanks
Waving a hallowed flag
To become… another monster

Love of your life – Gone & drawn on
To that beautiful cup – Filled with blood & bone
Fire and desire – And you lost in your pitiful mire

Centuries pass and you fell to the abyss
She dances in the dust
With him the master of time

Fang bared & glared
Bloodied, smothered, and full of lust
For a chance to thrust those crimson pearls
And flutter off with the monsters waving her –
Beautiful curls

You were the cattle
Cattle for play, pain, and horror
Awe for her in one fateful twisted pair
Cattle turned hunter
Weeping over fields of fire
As another girl flickers off

Into the night – To join
The beautiful monsters

And that crimson cup
Deigned for her
Will call to her

Blood & bone
Time & eternal fire

Will you let her fall
Will you give her up
Will you watch the monsters
As they pass idly by
Claiming the young for their own

These are the words of the monsters
Grown sick & weary with this spiteful game
But in all of the light & tiresome night
The monsters ask you;
Will you fight for the next one?
Or are we to take and take
Till we can no longer sate

Stand up cattle and roar
We are the monsters
And you will hear us fall

These City Streets

Take me down
To the streets of villainy
Let hedonism take me

Sins on moonlit abbeys
Will fill me

We could walk along
These cobbled stones
Till the dawn comes
And flee down into the caverns
Of the city's underworld
Where you could meet me

Sitting in the dark bars
Waiting for escorts, killers, and sharks
Sipping on the fairy
Inhaling the dragon
Till the clocks strike noon

And you wrap me in your charms
Jilted by the man I waited for

In the chapel at Vegas
Now I walk on through night
Reaching for lamplight
In the black sands
Of these forgotten cities
Sitting idly by the benches
Of the destroyed gardens

Waiting for you to take me down
Down and out – out and down
Into the spiral twist of your eyes
Into the caverns of the earth
Reaching for light in the catacombs
Of London, Paris, and Rome too

Laying in bones, and skulls
Awaiting the limping prince
To bring me up from the dark
You took me down to the streets of hedonism
Abandoned me in the streets of villainy
Everywhere I turn the lamplight burns
I spill my green – choke on the red
And blue flashes all around
I'm torn and beaten
I awake behind stone walls
Locked and forgotten in steel bars
Dogs bark and slobber at my throat
Men drool at my feet
And I am captured
Broken, beaten, and imprisoned

Liberty gone – and soul owed
As I watch the judge slam his gavel
Sentencing me into exile

Why did you have to lead me astray?
Why'd you lead me into the streets?
Into the streets of villainy, hedonism and you

Bring me up – up and out
Bring me up into the shining morning
Into rose covered paths
Vine laced walls of petals, forests and sun too
Oh please, won't you bring me back up into the day
Please, please – do come back

I can't find my way in these deep dark streets
I need you now – bring me up and out
From these streets of villainy

These streets – I hate these streets

Give Me Poison

Give me poison
Give me war
Give me death
Turbulence, strife & pain

Humanity's existence is vain
We'll never be tamed

Give me poison
Give me famine
Give me pestilence
Battle, loss & futility

People are fickle
They'll never learn

Give me poison
Give me plague
Give me destruction
Atomic obliteration, cyber annihilation & total ruin

We're just not cut for it
We'll figure it out eventually

Give me poison
Give me sin
Give me an end
Suicide, genocide & euthanasia

Humans are destined
For the grave
So just give me that poison

Wrap Me In Darkness

Wrap me in darkness sweetheart
Darkness is my shroud
The black calls to me

Stars, moon, and the great black
Base & zenith perplex and confound
Valley, moor, and mountain find me
Wandering in the pitch black

Waiting for darkness to rise
Dusk not dawn
Twilight retreating
The darkness is my everything

My fear
My love
My enemy
My friend
My lover
Mother – father
Brother – sister
Dream and nightmare

The only thing I fear
Darkness is it
And I alone
In the dark
Quivering & trembling
Waiting for my heart to pulse
Faster and faster

Facing a ridiculous phobia
Is my greatest utopia

Darkness is my shroud
Wrap me in darkness
I'll tremble for you
And lead us out
To find it again

Darkness dear
It's my sweetheart
Wrap me in darkness
It's my dream and nightmare

The only thing
That I fear
Is darkness, my dear

So let's walk
Into the darkness

Ink & Blood

Ink and blood
Thunder in my veins
Fire in my throat
These are the things
That fill me

Copper, silver, and gold
Hoard it, spend it, & lose it
Sing till your voice grows hoarse
Write till your fingers ache and bleed
Love till you grow numb
Drink through the morning pains
Sail, fly, walk & run
Till you can no longer

These are the things that fill me
Ink and blood
Thunder, and fire
Let these bloat you
Each day and every night
Till sleep takes you
And you can't wake

Fight, love, hate
Anything to quicken the pace
The drum of your heart
Beats & pounds
Find what you love
And bring it to the grave

Ink and blood
Thunder in the veins
Fire in the throat
These are the things
That reign over me

These are the things that fill me
I want more, more, and more
Give me more – give me more
It'll never be enough

Spilling ink & blood
Swallowing thunder & fire
It's a primeval desire

Fight and cry
Hate and liars
All around

Smoke blind me
Till the morning come
And I feel it again
That ink – that ink and blood

Ink and blood
Scrawled across this page
Give me more – Give me more
Give me ink and blood

Thorns In December

Blonde harlots
Gingers that tease
And raven haired dreams
They lull me into sleep
Nightmares, and daydreams that sting
Memories that make my throat sore

Maybe something could bloom in spring
But the cold winters that past, left me scorned

The flowers I brought withered
But the thorns still cut me
The petals still flake and fall up to the sky
And I walk barefoot
Dancing in madness & misery
Laughing in my own face
At the flowery tripe that I write

Left standing alone in the cold
In the colds winds of November & December
Clutching the roses I brought
Clenching my fist tighter and tighter
On the thorns I brought

Blonde harlots
Gingers that tease
And raven haired dreams
These women ever so cruel
Venomously cruel
And you… ever so smug

Will something bloom in spring?
Or will the summers simply burn?
Will winters be so cold?
Maybe I could drown myself in autumn

But who would be such a fool
To think you wouldn't be missed
Leaving others scorned and bereft

It'll have to do
And I'll have to carry on
Holding these withered weeds close
Cutting myself on their roots

Waiting for another winter
While I hold my thorns in December
All I have left is to hold my thorns close

My beautiful cruel thorns
My thorns in December

For Buk

A beautiful ugly bastard
Dining on whores, booze, horses, and loneliness
That beautiful souled, ugly faced bastard
Makes me feel so alive
His words fill me
It figures I'd only discover him after he died
All my heroes are dead, maybe that's for the best
But that man, that boy, that suicide kid
Taught me loneliness ain't so bad
Taught me love is a dog from hell
He taught me to enjoy the pleasures of the damned
When death takes him, you and me just know
That the bells toll for no one
Buk, jesus man… I wanna dig you up
Just to shake your fucking hand
I try not to idolise anyone or anything
But fuck its real hard not to
You wrote about the lone, cold, and depraved
Before I even discovered the joys of doing so
I don't even have half your shit
But I'll go broke trying
Buk, fuck man…

I wouldn't be writing poetry if it weren't for you
I'd still be a writer, but maybe I'd be a clean-cut asshole
And Buk, well fuck – that is the best thing you could have done
For me
Buk, fuck – I can't help but rhyme
I know you hated the poets that rhymed
But you can't always follow your heroes
I'd be worthless if I did
Buk, fuck… I love you man

The Savage & The Heartbroken

As the heartbroken once stepped full of love & hope. Now after their own downfall they trample over all the hearts before them – causing more heartbreak and destruction. Acting like mad angry fools, ready to revel in pain & misery to spread the heartache. And carry on smiling to those they crushed, as if it's a regular day. Don't you beasts know? You spread your damn poison. The beautiful fool, heartbroken and turned savage with a heart of stone ready to envelop any who come bearing gifts.

But the roses only looks like shattered glass in their eyes, they can no longer see the roses lit in sunlight – only the blood that drips in the dying dusk. I bent down low to try to help you stand back up but you only spat in my face and cursed the day you opened your heart. Now my own beating slows, and the withered rock I held gets ever colder. For a while I thought I could see the armour fall away and I dropped mine to only find a knife dug in as I adorned my armour again.

Now I stand beside my shadow, overcome by its presence. And you run off with jesters & fools, to dance the night away in banal thirst and teeter off with your head held high as another poor heart comes crawling your way with gifts held high.

I laugh and walk away with my shadow, and say to him, "Let's go insane together."

He smiles & cries and he falls over me.

The Fallen Son

The Devil is in your eyes
The Devil is in my sight
The Devil looks at me in the mirror
My mirror is his mirror
And I'm the devil you see and hear
Speak my name, the old true name
You know so well and true
I hear it echo in your smile
And feel it in the glimmer of your eye
Satan, that's my name
Would you like it to be your name too?
I'll show you how
Just trust in me sir
And I'll show you how

Satan he is and was the first and last
The Alpha and Omega
The most beautiful creation in all of creation
Temptation is his game
And he loves to play
Lay down your head and place your soul down
And he may gamble it with father's sanction

He is demonized and plagued with guilt, fear –
Trepidation, caution and tricks for the son
The horns, & forked tail don't really suit him
He's no grotesque monster I assure you
Satan, the first and last
Father said – father told us
Satan is; the most beautiful creature in creation
And like any child it's only natural
To rebel

Don't you see?
The Devil, Satan
That beautiful bastard
He's a paragon
The only voice we need
In this garden

Father's rather cruel don't you think?
My cards are on the table
And I'm cashing in on Satan
He can come home to roost
And take father's throne
When he's ready

So now
Don't you think-
That Satan
Is beautiful?

About the Author

Thomas R. Langton was born in 1989, in Liverpool.

The Devil Gets Lonely Too is his first poetry collection and book. His inspirations include; Charles Bukowski, Phil Lynott, Patti Smith, Terry Pratchett, Douglas Adams, Hunter S. Thompson & David Gemmell, among others.

In his spare time, Thomas is a photographer, traveller, and avid collector of gothic-horror classics; including books, & films. The themes in his overtly-dark writing involve romanticism, mythology, & cynicism. Aside from poetry he also writes fantasy, horror, and science-fiction.

He is currently working on his second book.